Purple Ronnie's

Little

KAMA SUTRA

by Purple Ronnie

First published 2004 by Boxtree
an imprint of PanMacmillan Publishers Ltd.
20 New Wharf Road
London N1 9RR

www.panmacmillan.com

Associated companies throughout the world

ISBN 0 7522 7270 5

9 8 7 6 5 4 3

A CIP catalogue record for this book is
available from the British Library

Text by Giles Andreae
Illustrations by Janet Cronin
Printed and Bound in Hong Kong

The Wheelbarrow

A very good one if you like a bit of outdoor action

Special Tip
Walk along slowly and you can get the weeding done at the same time

Rumpy-Pump Express

The jiggety-jig of the train track is all you need to really get you going

Special Tip

It is best to do this in-between stations as you never know who's about to come and sit next to you

Difficulty Rating: ☆ ☆
Pleasure Rating: ♡ ♡ ♡

The Lazy Boy

The man does not need to move at all. Both his hands are kept free for eating chips and changing the T.V. channel

Special Tip

The girl is also free to do her nails and to read mags

Difficulty Rating: ☆

Pleasure Rating: ♡

Fresh Air Frolic

Nothing feels nicer than the cool breeze blowing around your bottom

Special Tip

Watch out for stinging nettles, red ants and dogs running off with your undies

Difficulty Rating: ☆
Pleasure Rating: ♡ ♡

The Acrobat

Almost impossible unless you've had years of training. Not much fun even if you have

Special Tip

There is no point attempting this unless loads of people are watching.
For show-offs only.

Sheepskin Shag

An absolute classic and very romantic

Special Tip

Candles, a roaring log fire and some soppy music can make this even more dreamy

Warning: Be careful not to fall off the rug or you might get carpet burns on your bottom

Difficulty Rating: ☆

Pleasure Rating: ♡ ♡ ♡

The Footy Fan

This position will allow both of you to watch the match without getting in each other's way

Special Tip

Extra stimulation can be achieved if you jump up and down when a goal is scored

Difficulty Rating: ☆
Pleasure Rating: ♡ ♡

Dashboard Diddler

A brilliant way of testing out your man's driving skills

Tip for Men

Be responsible - keep your eyes on the road and you hands on the wheel at all times

Beach-Side Bonk

The sound of waves crashin
on the shore can be
really sexy

Special Tips

Make sure you put a towel
down first or you will get
very scratchy parts

Watch out for crabs

Shuffle in the Shower

A very good one as no-one has to sleep in the wet patch afterwards

Special Tip

It is best to use a wall for support because if you slip on the soap you could have a nasty acciden

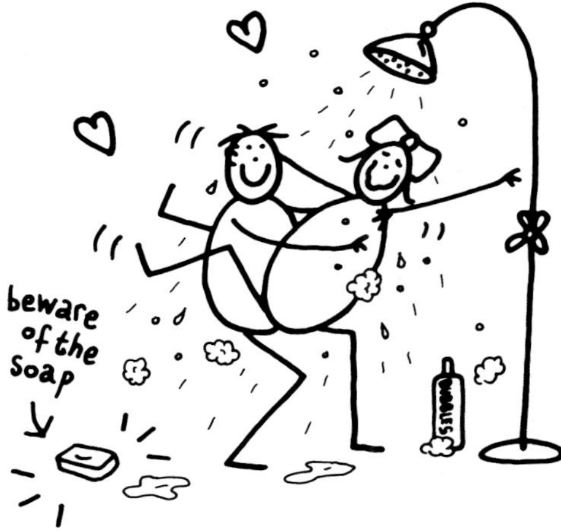

Difficulty Rating: ☆ ☆

Pleasure Rating: ♡ ♡

Good Vibrations

Set your washing machine to spin then sit on top of it and let the machine do the rest

Special Tip

Put some heavy towels into the machine to really get it rocking

The Fat Boy

Girls can enjoy this position even if there's a giant beer belly wobbling on the mattress next to them

Warning: Make sure the m stays lying down on his side. If he rolls over on top of you you might get squashed

Chocolate Heaven

No girl can resist chocolate, so this can be a great way for a man to break the ice

Warning: Do not attempt this on the carpet or you will be washing it out for ages

Madame Spanky

Some men like nothing more than a good hard spank on the bottom with a hairbrush

Tips for Girls

If the man starts sucking his thumb and calling you mummy it might be time to start looking for someone else

Difficulty Rating: ☆
Pleasure Rating: ♡ ♡

Mile High Moaner

Aeroplane toilets are so small that the girl can use both walls for support

Warning: It can be quite hard for two people to go into an aeroplane lav together without being spotted, so try to think up a good excuse firs

Difficulty Rating:
Pleasure Rating:

Quickie in the Kitchen

V. Useful if you just can't wait to get to the bedroom Could be a good one if the romantic dinner has gone down well

Special Tip

It is a good idea to clear the table first

slide

crash

plonk

splat

Difficulty Rating: ☆
Pleasure Rating: ♡ ♡

The Bungey Bouncer

For thrill seekers only.
Do not attempt this
unless you are utterly
mad

Special Tip

It is best to take a
sick bag with you just
in case

Difficulty Rating: ☆ ☆ ☆
Pleasure Rating: ♡

Wash and Go

A very warm and cosy
position with plenty
of rude slurping noises

Special Tip

A great one to try if you
haven't got time to shower
afterwards as you can wash
each other while you're
Doing I

giggle • curly wigy • steam • scrub • splosh • bubbles • shampoo

Difficulty Rating: ☆ ☆
Pleasure Rating: ♡ ♡

The Tree Hugger

A great way to get in touch with nature and Do It at the same time

Tip for Girls

It is best to keep your shirt on or you will get a very sore back

Difficulty Rating: ☆ ☆
Pleasure Rating : ♡

The Lager Lover

Lager Lovers can do this without even needing to put down their beer

Warning: If your beer belly is very big you might not be able to get close enough to do this

Lust in the Lav

Great if you fancy a quickie at a party and someone else is using the bedroom

Warning: Be careful not to fall into the toilet

Difficulty Rating: ☆ ☆
Pleasure Rating: ♡ ♡

The Tied-Up Teaser

A great one for the girl who wants to be totally in control

__Warning__: Some girls find this position so satisfying that they don't untie their men for several days afterward